Thinking & Living

Thinking & Living

By Manchester Boddy

designed & illustrated by
Gene Galasso

THE C. R. GIBSON COMPANY ■ NORWALK, CONNECTICUT

Contents

Introduction

The author, Manchester Boddy, was born in a small homestead on the slopes of the Cascade Mountains in western Washington. During his youth he worked as a dairy hand and as a miner in the zinc and lead mines of western Idaho.

As a result of these early endeavors he was able to attend Washington State College and the University of Montana. His early career included door to door sales work with Encyclopedia Britannica and the New York Times Current History Magazine. He also served in various capacities in the book and magazine publishing field and had the experience of serving overseas in the U.S. Infantry. During the last quarter century of his career he was Publisher and Editor of the Los Angeles Daily News.

The thoughts presented in "Thinking and Living" are reflections upon the thoughts and concerns which entered the mind of the author as he passed through the various stages of his life. From his humble beginning one can well appreciate that over the years he was faced with many decisions and difficulties, perhaps even frequent discouragement. All adversities were overcome, as his zest for living taught him to face the future and develop a positive philosophy of life as portrayed in this volume.

Thinking & Living

A little group of old-timers were enjoying themselves with tales of the days that used to be. One of the party told the ever-new story of the great San Francisco fire that followed the quake of 1906. He told of lucky breaks and deeds of heroism. But mostly he told of the terrific setbacks experienced by successful men and women.

"But," asked one of his listeners, "did you ever consider the effect it had upon the unsuccessful folk? The thousands who had overdrawn checking accounts at the banks, the many more who had notes due that couldn't be paid and the thousands of others who were stalling off landlords, butchers, bakers and other money takers?"

The question was well put. At least seven people out of every ten are burdened with worries and cares which often drive them nearly to desperation until at times they would welcome an earthquake or any other catastrophe—even war—that might reduce others to their circumstances.

Everyone knows, of course, that worry is an unhealthy condition of the mind. It feeds upon energy and produces nervous, irritable wrecks who cannot get along with themselves or their neighbors. Describing the evils of worry is easy, but useless. No one wants it, least of all those afflicted with it. Neither is it fair or helpful to dismiss the subject merely by saying one should avoid doing the things that cause worry.

Worry follows closely upon the heels of fear. Not the kind of fear that comes from the sudden threat of physical danger, but a kind that is born in the imagination, fed and nourished by constant thought. As a finger penetrated by a splinter brings to its aid an army of white corpuscles to fight and banish the splinter, so does the mind afflicted with fear bring to its aid currents of nervous activity. The name of this activity is worry.

While imagination is the well-spring in which all human accomplishments originate, it is also the source of fear. The worrier has an active imagination. His imagination is out of control and is allowed to gather its food from the thought currents of the air, the newspapers, magazines, books, motion pictures, radio, television, gossip, and from many other sources.

Ridding our minds of worry does not mean that we are going to ignore our responsibilities, crawl out from under the load we have saddled upon ourselves or have had saddled upon us by others. Neither does it mean that we are to shrug our shoulders in resignation to whatever fate the future has in store for us.

Two simple little exercises will help us get rid of worry. First, we must constantly work at making our thoughts, our actions and our motives harmonize with our consciences. Perhaps we will find that our standard of measurement is not our conscience at all, but rather is based upon what other people do and what other people seem to think is all right. It will help if we remember that each individual is a world within himself. Let's not starve our own natural development by patterning our inner life after the outward life of others.

It is useless to go further unless we can start now and gradually make our every thought, action and motive harmonize with our inner self. This exercise will bring immediate results.

The next exercise is more difficult. It consists of harmonizing with those nearest to us. We must not wait until we arrive at our respective jobs to start this exercise. Start it at home; try harmonizing with the mood in which you find the other members of the family. In all seriousness, this is the surest way to complete life satisfaction that we know of. Each of us at least can try it. Taken in conjunction with the first exercise, it is certain to bring rich rewards.

When we set out to harmonize ourselves with those nearest at hand, let's mean to do exactly that. If the wife or husband is tired, cross or nervous, let's not accept this unfortunate but common condition as a challenge and immediately develop a counter mood of our own that will only create taut nerves and discord. Let's honestly try to make our presence a comfort and help.

Few of us ever give ourselves the treat of really trying to bring comfort and happiness to our own home folk by harmonizing with them. So many times we think that paying the rent, buying the food and that sort of thing is all that we should be expected to do. Actually, when we reason this way, we are putting the cart before the horse. For any person who can live in harmony with himself and, at the same time, in harmony with his own family, and who thus can banish discord, not by the rule of might or a loud voice, but by practicing unselfish consideration, soon will be endowed with a personality and ability that will be rewarded with undreamed-of success in the world.

Each individual has a slightly different list of things he is worrying about, but, in the main, each list will have the same characteristics. For the sake of convenience we will call the list of things we worry about—our troubles.

Let us look these troubles squarely in the face. An old philosopher was wont to say that if we all could take our troubles and put them on a great common pile from which we later would be compelled to take our choice, we would seize the first opportunity to steal up silently to the pile and take back our own.

In honestly facing our troubles, let us try to consider their actual value—not the value our imagination has put upon them. Have you ever tried listening to someone else's troubles? Have you noticed how imaginary and sometimes trivial they appear to you, but how real and terrible they appear to the person who has them?

Your troubles are relative. For instance, suppose you should, upon arrival at your work this morning, be handed a telegram telling of the grave illness of some loved one. Instantly this new worry would supplant all others you are carrying. You would feel selfish and ashamed if you continued to think only of your own troubles; you would concentrate on the new one. And if something you could do would save the life of the loved one, you would do it. You would rise to new heights and be supported by a new strength that you hardly knew you had.

Then, suppose it was discovered that the telegram was a mistake; a terrible mixup of names and did not concern you at all. With a sigh of relief you would take up your regular course of living. But you would have had, for an instant, an insight into the relative value of the regular load of troubles you have been carrying. Something went on in your mind. That was all.

Recently a party of novices made a trip into the Mojave desert. Stopping at a spring, they filled their empty desert bags and drank. A group of men decided to play a trick. Rushing up to the people at the spring they exclaimed that the water was poisoned and was, in fact, the famous poison spring that had killed so many early travelers. The jokesters suddenly realized that their crude joke was having an unexpected result. Several in the party fell desperately ill, and only by heroic work were their lives saved.

What happened? Again, something went on in the mind.

The thing that went on in the minds of these people, and

the thing that would make you respond to the alarming telegram, is the greatest power in the world. If we are to banish worry and get the most out of life, we must learn how to harness this power and make it work for us. This we can do. And to a greater or lesser extent, every successful person—whether he knows it or not—relies entirely upon this power.

Power of Imagination

In the homestead country of western Washington, where the writer was reared, there was a "no account" boy who wouldn't work around the place and wouldn't study at school. The boy's name was William and everyone called him Bill. Bill loved to fish and hunt. He would walk miles through the hills without food or rest in quest of game. When the fishing season opened, Bill knew the best holes and was first to bring home a string of trout. Otherwise, Bill seemed to be a total loss.

No one, it seemed, could do anything for him. Then one day a stranger came into the hills. He was a young engineer, sent to secure data for a great water power project. Far out in the woods the young engineer met Bill. The two became fast friends. The young engineer told Bill alluring stories of the life of an engineer. He pictured adventurous trips into little known mountain countries, and dangerous expeditions into the wilds of Mexico.

Suddenly Bill wanted to be an engineer. He wanted this new objective just as earnestly and enthusiastically as he had previously wanted to hunt and fish.

From then on, there was no holding Bill. Today he is one of the foremost mining engineers of the country.

Driving, scolding and punishing couldn't budge Bill one step. His imagination pulled him like a magnet, and he overcame all obstacles.

We are all, in the main, like Bill. We may speak of duty—and strain, push and pull at what we call will power. But when all is said and done, we usually do what we want to do. Consider this carefully, for we are about to add a third exercise to the two previously given.

Your worries, or troubles, as we decided to call them, are bound to end in one of two ways. Either things will come out all right, or there will be some of the terrible consequences you now fear.

Very well. Our objective is to see that things come out all right. If you are diligently practicing the first two exercises, you may start this one, and your trouble will vanish just as surely as the gray mist is dissipated by the early morning sun.

Instead of allowing your imagination to picture the terrible consequences and the worst side of your troubles, start now to picture the joy and happiness that will be yours when your troubles are over. Picture your every action, repeat the very words you will use and the very manner in which you will act when you reach the hour, or day, when the climax of your troubles is due. Be very definite and exact about it. Your picture must be just as definite and certain as if it were being projected upon a screen before your eyes.

You will be amazed to find how exactly the actual events will coincide with the mental picture you have created. Don't stop to wonder how it will happen, and don't hold mental reservations or doubts. Live with your picture, dream it, and never for an instant allow the dark picture to form in your mind. Don't create a negative picture. That is to say, don't picture the bad side and say to yourself:

"This won't happen." Because if you do this, it will happen.

At this point the temptation is to say: "Now, you see, I've tried this new way and it doesn't work." If we do say this, and quit trying, we are hopelessly lost. If we work diligently and intelligently at the task nearest at hand in accordance with our three essential exercises, we must accept whatever happens with the assurance that we are making progress. Presently we will find ourselves closer by far to our objectives than if we allow a wall-like obstacle across our path to discourage us.

The wall—our trials and tribulations—can be made to serve a useful purpose, even as the grief we are sometimes called upon to bear. It is far better to believe so. No one has accomplished great things in the world who has not traveled a road beset with many pitfalls, thorns and stones. But like the adverse wind against which the skillful mariner brings his vessel into the harbor, so are our discouragements, disappointments and setbacks. And like the mariner, we, too, may proceed against these adversities and gain our objectives.

From now on, then, regardless of all adversities, we constantly will strive to live in perfect harmony with our inner selves. We will practice the most useful and beautiful art in the world—the art of living in harmony with other people, especially the people who are our own. We will create a picture in our minds of the course ahead and we will, as a natural consequence, find ourselves following true to this course.

Harmony with Inner Selves

Our capacity to comprehend the principles already outlined is measured by the extent to which we recognize our troubles, and the amount of relief and benefit we receive from the use of the principles is measured by our capacity for worrying and suffering.

Our Creator has endowed each of us with certain powers. We may use these powers for good or evil. If our spiritual lives are starved and our hours and days are spent in constant or intermittent worry, it is not a sign that we do not have the capacity or ability to comprehend and use the principles we have studied thus far. On the contrary, it is evidence that we do have both the capacity and the power to comprehend and use them. We are allowing the power we have to be used in a wrong way, that is all.

One afflicted with worry or trouble will find it difficult at first to reverse his order of thinking. He will constantly be tempted to cling to certain thought habits that have

been developed through the years. Before he can live in harmony with his inner self, he will need to free his conscience or inner self from a number of things.

When an electric current does not travel to the light bulb, the room is plunged into darkness. Instantly we search along the wire for the cause. We do not question the existence of the current, nor do we question the fact that it can travel along the wire and light the bulb.

Neither should we question the existence of our inner spiritual power. We should look for obstacles that are preventing its development. Often these obstacles are prejudice, hatred, envy, vindictiveness and, above all, a tendency to look for evil in others—to hope that others may get into trouble so that our own position will seem, by comparison, good or at least tolerable.

We cannot hope to remove all these obstacles at once, but we can regulate our thoughts and make an earnest effort toward doing so. And this effort, in itself, constitutes the exercise of living in harmony with our inner selves.

One reason we find it difficult to live in harmony with our inner self is because our physical self is constantly trying to run away from our spiritual self.

Perhaps some of us have never slowed down long enough to contemplate why we have acquired the habit of seeking excitement; why we are so anxious to be on the go, and why our chief desire is to surround ourselves with all manner of diversions that money can buy.

We do these things to excess as a substitute for living well-balanced lives. That is to say, our physical lives have received attention while our spiritual lives have had little or none.

Yet all around us we see evidence that physical excitement alone offers only temporary relief. Interest lags for the chronic playboy because he must be entertained by artificial means. The novelty and excitement furnished by artificial means soon wears off and something more is needed.

The end is nearly always the same. Either he becomes blasé and indifferent to everything and consequently irritable and unhappy, or he becomes progressively braver at each subsequent debauch until he finds himself pursuing a course of modified or outright licentiousness, which ends in misery.

But all the while he has prevented his spiritual life from developing. And since his spiritual life has not been developed, it is folly suddenly to call upon it to supplant his well-entrenched habits of seeking happiness in the turmoil and babble of the crowds.

Each of us needs to live a simple, well-balanced life in which our physical self can harmonize with our inner self.

And an excellent test to apply to ourselves in living toward this end is whether or not the things we do by choice, and the things we want to do, contribute to our physical and spiritual growth alike.

As we read accounts of the early days in California we are thrilled with the tales of men who braved the elements and fought their way through all manner of hardships to the time when their efforts were crowned with victory in the form of gold dust.

Strangely enough, we hear little of what the men did with their wealth; both those who tell the tales and those who listen to them are interested only in living over the hardships and perils of the times.

Very soon the early prospectors learned the difference between real gold and "fools' gold." Both have much the same appearance. If anything, the deceptive little yellow flakes of fools' gold have more the appearance of the real thing than gold itself.

When we come to the end of our miner's story and read that his gold dust was all that he had hoped for and was safely put away, we call the story a romance. If, after the miner's struggles were over, we find that he had returned with bags of worthless fools' gold, we call the story a tragedy. It would be a tragedy because the miner had spent his all and endured hardships and struggles for nothing.

So it is with our lives. In attempting to point the way to live without worry and to achieve a life of accomplishments, we do not hold out the hope that the better life will not be as strenuous and as filled with problems as is the life fraught with worry and misery.

We set forth the truth that the journey can be made; that, gradually but certainly, even our problems and hardships will contribute to the enrichment of our lives, and illuminate our twilight years with pleasure and contentment. Neither will we need to wait for the journey's end to find our reward. We will experience it every day.

Each of us should make certain that we are not gathering fools' gold as we go along instead of the real values that make life worth the living. If we are gathering fools' gold, ·our life experience will be no less a tragedy than was the story of the unfortunate miner.

Many will immediately recognize this truth. The important thing, however, will be for us to determine which is fools' gold and which is true.

As the prospector must learn to distinguish between real values and the quantities of fools' gold that sparkle so alluringly in the sands of the streams, so must we, who would realize the most from life, learn to distinguish between false and real values.

This does not require study. Neither does it require a great deal of help from others. The prospector took his findings to the assay office and learned the·value of what he had. We carry our own assay office wherever we go. And everything we do, everything we think—and indeed our very motives—pass through this assay office whether we want them to or not.

This assay office is our inner self. It invariably tells us the truth. We can either accept the truth or reject it. The prospector has the same privilege. He may continue hoarding his fools' gold. It is much easier to acquire and soon bulks very large in his pouch.

Very often we are not willing to accept the verdict of our own assay office. We take our thoughts, plans and deeds to someone else and ask him to assay them for us. We do this because we want him to tell us that they have real life values and are not merely pieces of fools' gold, as our own assay office tells us they are. We go from one assay office to the other until we find one that is willing to tell us what we want most to hear.

This is the course we take in fooling ourselves. It soon becomes a habit and we depend less and less upon our own assay office. Of course, no one can do our assaying for us. A thought, or a motive or an act may be right for one and wrong for another. When we judge others we are doing their assaying for them; when they judge us they are doing our assaying for us. In both cases the unfortunate results are the same.

Many of us long for a more interesting life—one filled with big events and outstanding achievements. We are tired of the petty worries and the humdrum tribulations that come with bare existence. We fear monotony will drive us mad. This is just another way of saying that we crave more of the raw material of life. Each of us has a complete, well-ordered equipment for handling the raw material of life. The quantity we handle depends entirely upon our ability to handle, as we should, that which inevitably comes to us each day.

So, instead of longing for more, we should concentrate on handling what we have. We should clear our assay office for work. We should learn to respect its decisions faithfully and at all times. Our physical life quickly will harmonize with our inner development, and more and more we will find ourselves actually living the mental pictures that we have formed of the course that lies ahead.

Hidden Powers

The girls behind the counter were unusually busy for such a hot day. For the most part the customers were patient and courteous, which made the actions of one, who was not, very conspicuous.

This woman elbowed her way to the counter and demanded immediate attention. It was easy to see that she could not be satisfied. Yet she persisted in irritating the clerks and imposing upon the other customers.

After she had left the counter we heard one weary clerk say to another: "What a superiority complex that woman has!"

It is true that this unfortunate woman, like many of us, has a complex. But it is an inferiority, not a superiority, complex—as we shall see.

One reason it is so difficult to live a well-balanced life, free from worry and rich in accomplishment, is because so many of us have an inferiority complex.

The source of the inferiority complex is a feeling within us that we are inferior. To overcome this feeling we do and say things that tend to make us appear superior. Hence, the woman who annoyed her fellow customers and imposed upon the clerks assumed a superior attitude to counterbalance the annoying feeling of inferiority that constantly harassed her from within.

The inferiority complex has many ways of showing itself. It is frequently reflected in our overbearing treatment of those who serve us.

It is particularly evident in the manner in which we drive our motor cars. So many who drive a small, out-of-date machine make up for the inferiority they feel by hogging the road, beating others to the crossing, cutting in, and in many other ways practicing bad road manners.

Conversation almost always betrays the presence of the inferiority complex. Observe an informal gathering and you will notice that among those present are many who engage in animated discussions concerning subjects they really know little about. They do this because they wish to convince themselves and others that they have superior knowledge or information.

We cannot live in perfect harmony with others until we eliminate the inferiority complex.

The way to eliminate the inferiority complex is to follow the very simple advice, "Be yourself."

And if, while we are following it, we are at the same time seeking to live in harmony with our inner selves, we very quickly will develop a personality that will achieve for us the position in life we now seek through the fraudulent practices inspired by the inferiority complex.

We will be aided and encouraged in following the thought expressed in this little book by realizing how seriously and earnestly intelligent men and women everywhere are recognizing the great values and the amazing possibilities of the proper uses of the mind.

Recently a New York philanthropist announced that he was considering a plan to create a $10,000,000 endowment for the betterment of mankind. A great New York newspaper conducted a contest for the best plan for using the huge sum.

More than 100,000 plans were submitted. In the end, the prize was given to the man who suggested the establishment of a foundation in the field of mental hygiene. This is only one of many recent acknowledgments of the vast importance of the power of thought, and the full and correct use of the mind.

In the course of a conversation a man utterly forgot a name that he knew as well as his own. His listener said: "Never mind. It will come to you." But the man continued to struggle with his memory in a desperate effort to call forth the elusive name.

Again his friend said: "You never will recall the name until you forget about it and think of something else."

"I suppose I might as well," replied the perplexed man, "but I know the name as well as I know my own."

The conversation turned to other things. Half an hour later, in the middle of a sentence, the missing name suddenly crashed into the man's mind and he fairly shouted it forth, although it had nothing whatever to do with the thought or conversation of the moment.

A practical, hard-headed engineer was charged with running a preliminary line for a projected railroad. In the course of his work he encountered a seemingly insurmountable problem. His employers were demanding immediate results. After struggling with his problem for many hours without avail, he deliberately dismissed the entire matter from his mind and went fishing.

A few days later the solution to his problem, clear and well defined, came to his mind. How was the solution worked out, and where did it come from?

Each of us can recall similar examples. We say we "sleep over" our problems and the answers come to us. Of course, this isn't what we do at all. We really put them somewhere and then seemingly forget them. Many people, upon retiring for the night, set the desired time of awakening definitely in their minds—and invariably awaken at precisely the time set.

There are many scientific terms used in describing the part of us that does these things for us. We do not need to know these terms. We do not need to confuse our minds with any scientific explanations of any of the many theories and ideas that have been advanced concerning them.

All we need to do, for the present, is to acknowledge that we do have a workshop that occasionally does things for us without conscious effort on our part.

We well remember the first time a youngster in our neighborhood strung up a crude little telephone line, which was hooked on to some old discarded batteries. At last a faint sound came over the wire. The boy bounded about with glee, his eyes sparkled, and for a moment all he could say was: "It works! It works!"

Today, then, let us recall to mind the instances when the workshop that we know so little about has actually done things for us. It is enough to know, for the present, that such a workshop exists. Later on we will be amazed to find how much this workshop can do for us, and how easy it is for us to use it.

Harmony is the objective which all life seeks. All creation is harmony. Each individual, in his natural state, is a collection of parts that work in harmony each with the other. Hence, our inner workshop, as we call it, has a capacity that harmonizes with, and is in exact proportion to, the part of us that we call our mind.

It follows, then, that each individual has an inner workshop of sufficient proportions to serve his full requirements. And it follows, also, that our workshop is capable of accomplishing any task that our mind is capable of conceiving.

It is extremely important that we study this thought carefully. To make it clearer: We have observed that many individuals upon retiring at night can charge their minds with the exact time for awakening the next morning. And, precisely at the time set, they do awake.

Now, if the individual could not comprehend or picture the exact time, he would give his workshop hazy, indefinite instructions—or no instructions at all—and in return would experience hazy, indefinite results.

But the character of results obtained would mean nothing to him, for he would have no conception of better results by which to measure them.

In the study of how to solve our perplexing problems, we must realize that our inner self, our workshop, is the source from which the final solutions will come; and that its capacity for solving our problems is in exact proportion to our ability to conceive them. But we should realize further that our worries are not problems.

Accepting the truth that each of us has an inner mind or workshop that harmonizes and works in conjunction with our other mental faculties, our immediate concern is to learn how to use this powerful agency most effectively.

Cecil John Rhodes, one of the outstanding empire builders of his time, led a strenuous life of action. In fighting savages, helping desperate pioneers, and in carrying on a great colonization project, part of it concurrently with the Boer war and trouble in England, he had ample opportunity to worry.

"In the midst of all these problems," he once said to a friend, "I find relaxation, peace and comfort in dreaming my future plans." Part of his dreams included the Rhodes scholarship plan, which has long since been a reality.

Rhodes could have spent his time worrying. He had plenty to worry about. But he knew that worrying would never solve his problems. There is a vast difference between having perplexing problems and even grievous cares, and worrying. Problems can, as we have seen, be solved. Even our cares and responsibilities can honorably be carried with much compensating spiritual value to us, but worry demoralizes our forces and prevents us from solving our problems and from carrying our responsibilities as we should.

Rhodes, whether he realized it or not, was using his inner workshop to the fullest extent.

A Philosophy of Life

That portion of our mind which we call into use when we think, or add figures, or read a book, is the guardian of the inner workshop and passes into it the conceptions that are later to be developed into practical existence. To get the most out of the workshop it is essential that we examine carefully that which goes into it.

We have, we will say, a definite period of time in which to meet an obligation. If we fail to meet it, there will be certain bad consequences. We know what these consequences will be. They are very real in our mind, and almost without our meaning to do so, we create a mental picture of them and dwell upon them at great length.

When we do this we are creating a definite thought in our mind which is transmitted to our inner workshop and developed there. The evil picture has a power over us, and we wish we could banish it from our minds. But there is only one way to do this. We must create a picture to take its place.

The instruction that our obligation must be met is firmly implanted in our inner mind and consequently there comes to us a constant reminder which, in turn, takes the form of a mental picture. This should be a picture of our meeting the obligation. Never mind how. If there is no plain way open and we have been unable to find a way, leave the entire matter with the inner workshop.

But let us not put a negative thought right along with it. While the plan is being worked out inside our inner mind we can help by continually making the mental picture of our meeting the obligation vivid and real. Soon we will firmly believe in it. And the amazing thing is that it will come true.

Says a friend: "Your theories are fascinating. I agree with them and wish I could use them. But there the thing stops. I am afraid that just hearing about them or reading them isn't enough and, after all, I can't change myself, can I?"

This friend undoubtedly expresses a thought that has formed, or is forming, in many minds. It is an interesting question and one that should be answered adequately.

We have referred to that part of our being which we call our mind, or our brain. We have discussed another part of us that sometimes is referred to as the inner mind or, as we called it, the inner workshop. Also we have found in our study that the inner workshop develops in proportion to development of our outer mind, or brain.

This question naturally presents itself: Do our minds control us, or do we control our minds? An interesting question indeed!

Let us say we have an extremely important engagement for six o'clock this evening to which we have been looking forward for a long time. But we have certain routine work that must be done before six o'clock or we cannot keep the engagement. We apply ourselves to our task, which, let us say, consists of adding columns of figures. We work for a few minutes or for an hour, when, presently, a far-away look comes into our eyes, the figures fade, and we lapse into a day dream. Suddenly we realize what we are doing and say sternly to our mind: "You concentrate on these figures and get them added. No more wandering around until the job is finished."

Or, we look out of the window and see a figure that challenges our attention. Instantly our mind wishes to take command and desert the columns of figures. With great effort we sternly rebuke our mind and again set it to the task of adding figures. Finally, after much effort, our mind finishes its particular task.

In these two cases was the mind telling itself what to do? No. Our composite self—we—told the mind what to do. This "we" sometimes is called our ego. There are, in fact, many scientific words that describe it. All we need to know is that we can tell our brain to set to work and, moreover, we can see to it that it stays at work.

If we are to get the benefit in store for us from the use of the suggestions set forth in this book, we must assert our control over our mind and start exercising and disciplining it. So often we merely drift along before the whims and caprices of our mind, never exerting our authority over it and seldom, if ever, giving it regular exercise.

Recently I talked with a man who had just been released from a state prison.

"Do you think," he asked, "that it is possible after what I have gone through, to adjust myself to society, to get along with other people as if nothing had happened, and, maybe, get ahead in the world?"

This unfortunate had missed the great lesson that all must learn before the real satisfaction of living can be experienced.

"Your first step," I replied, "is to get in harmony with yourself. Every bargain you make, every thought you dwell upon, every secret plan you form in your mind is witnessed by your inner self, or conscience. The extent to which you harmonize with others and adjust yourself to society is measured entirely by your willingness and ability to harmonize with your inner self.

"If your unfortunate past has hurt you with yourself, then the damage will be carried on and hurt your relations with others. First, then, repair the damage that has been done to yourself. You have help at hand. This help will come from the only real friend you have in the wide world. This friend is your inner self.

"You may have slighted this friend, abused it and all but smothered it, but it has not deserted you. It has stood by you, faithful and true. It will praise you when all others condemn you. It will make you strong and capable when all manner of adversities descend upon you.

"It will comfort you and cause your heart to overflow
with the fullness of life when all else about you seems con-
fused and dark.

"Wherever you go, this friend goes with you. Even to
prison. And when everyone else deserts you, this friend
will stand by you and be the first to say: 'Together we can
make life worth living. Let's start now!' "

There are many kinds of prisons, but the ones that pun-
ish us most are the ones we build ourselves. Destructive
habits, worry, misery—these and many other prisons are
built slowly, an exceedingly small part at a time.

But each part, small as it is, is built over the protest of
our ever faithful friend. While we alone may build the
prison walls that surround us, our friend—our inner, spiritual self—alone can tear them down.

There is one asset that ranks higher than government
bonds, first mortgages, life insurance, or even pure gold.
It is a well-developed, sound philosophy of life.

Aside from being the most valuable asset a man can
possess, it is the one asset that any man may acquire. One
may inherit gold, social position and even a place of
power. He must create his own philosophy of life.

A well-rounded philosophy of life is a shock-absorber
that protects our delicate and sensitive natures from in-
jury when the going is rough and we come face to face
with the stark realities of life.

We need our own philosophy of life every day. We need
to develop it, to live it, and to make it so much a part of us

that it will sustain us when comes the inevitable day that brings us our greatest of all sorrows—the loss of a loved one.

When this sad day visits us, as indeed it will, there will be little else to comfort us than our own philosophy of life. The solicitous word of friends, the slight pause in the order of things, are all so inadequate, so lacking in the thing we need. Yet they are all that others can do for us. The burden is our own.

On such a day our philosophy of life needs to tell us that grief for the departed cannot bring him back; that really our grief is for our own loss, not his. For he has finished the course that we are yet to run. And when we understand that we are grieving over our own loss and our own plight —not his—we find it possible again to face life as it is, with the comforting knowledge that our loss has been repaid by a deeper insight into the true meaning of life, and the source from which it flows.

Our philosophy of life should displace hatreds and envy. It will assure us that we get out of life exactly what we earn, and it will point the true way of living from the false.

The opposite to a true philosophy of life is the habit of self-pity; the feeling that we are misunderstood and never get exactly as much as we have coming. Feeling sorry for ourselves is the first warning that we need to readjust our attitude toward life and develop a philosophy that has its foundation in the essential truth that we have within us the means of living the kind of a life that will help others as well as being a solace to ourselves.

Discouragement often comes from the feeling that others are endowed with powers or virtues that we do not possess. We toe the starting mark in our race for what we call success, but before we start, we see the many runners already nearing the goal.

Others seem to run the race so easily. They get a lift here, and they get a lift there, while we keep trudging along, stumbling, running in circles, making no headway at all.

Sometimes we think we even lose ground; that the course we run upon is not a straightaway track at all, but a huge treadmill that keeps us working hard just to save ourselves.

We want help. We turn to the many theories of life and to the many teachers who point the way. Every bit of advice that seems at all reasonable finds a welcome with us and we do our best to follow it. Yet we see no change in our position.

Finally we become convinced, like the helpless little squirrel in its treadmill cage, that there is no hope—and we ease up on our treading. We are hopelessly discouraged and ready to quit. We have trod so long in one place that we have worn a deep rut. We see others beside us treading as we once trod. Little by little we huddle closer in our rut and let the wheel carry us if it will. And it will— for a while. But the treadmill has a law of its own and sooner or later the rut we are in closes over us and we are forgotten.

When discouragement comes in, the satisfaction of living goes out. We speak much of the tragedies of war and of the victims of famines, pestilences and floods. And yet the tragedy of discouragement blights more lives and visits misery upon more people than ever feel the crushing heel of war or experience the ravages of pestilences and floods.

Society can minister to the needs of the victim of disaster, but the discouragement that steals its way into our heart snuffs out the flame that lights our eyes and furnishes energy to our steps. Others cannot relight the flame for us; it can only be lighted from within.

Opening Windows

How then, may we avoid discouragement? We once saw a beautiful yellow and red tanager that was taken from his home in the chaparral and placed in a large glass cage. The little bird flew straight for the nearest light, but struck the glass with such force that he fell stunned to the bottom of the cage.

How many times are we battered down by an invisible barrier that stands between us and our goal!

Discouragement can come only after we have tried to do something and failed. Therefore, we should first be certain that what we are trying to do is the thing we should be trying to do. And we should go beyond this and discover why we are trying to do anything at all. For back of every effort is a motive, and unless this motive is right, nothing that follows can be right.

If we are to avoid discouragement, we must first be sure that our purpose in life is born of motives that harmonize

with our inner, spiritual self, and is not a creature of un-worthy desires. This is a simple truth that we all may understand. Each of us has been given the one priceless, divine gift. The gift of life! Life is given to each of us for a purpose, as we shall see. There have been countless generations of lives like ours in the past, as there will be in the future.

Taken as a whole, these ever-recurring individual lives comprise the great stream of life that has flowed on through the ages. The course of this stream of life is de-termined by the lives of the individuals who comprise it. Each individual is a moral agent, free to develop his spirit-ual self, or to ignore it and seek the savor of life through essentially materialistic channels, purposes and actions.

Each life must learn for itself which course to follow. Discouragement and misery are stern reminders that we have chosen the wrong course. The warm glow of the heart that follows the act of kindness, the comforting satis-faction that compensates us for doing our duty—in short, the genuine feeling of strength and peace that comes to us when we are attuned with our inner self, assures us that we have chosen the right course.

If the right way of living were obvious and if its advan-tages were easily seen, everyone would follow it without delay, and the great stream of life would come to its final resting place.

No individual knowingly or willingly hurts himself. If he is hurt, it is because he sees but dimly, and has fallen into the wrong course which, to his distress, he finds is filled with thorns and jagged rocks.

Discouragement comes when he fails to realize why his path is thus beset, and when he believes it means that progress is not for him. He needs to know that the thorns and rocks are but reminders that he has chosen the wrong course.

He will find that the right course starts within himself and traverses the territory nearest at hand. When we postpone living in harmony with ourselves and with those immediately about us, justifying our postponement by convincing ourselves that we will start when we are in different circumstances, we are planting the seed of certain discouragement and misery. For a change in circumstances starts with a change within ourselves. Never before!

Often our desire to improve ourselves first takes the form of acquiring and developing what we think are virtues. True virtue carries its own reward and becomes an integral, natural part of us. Some of the things we think of as virtues have no intrinsic value whatever within themselves, but are merely external fixtures that we fasten on to ourselves because we think that by wearing them we will earn some particular reward that will not be given to others who, for one reason or another, do not wear them.

Virtues are personal adornments. Each of us must measure the values of his own virtues by the extent to which they enable him to grow spiritually through service to others. We are prone to regard the virtues we display as the precious jewels of our particular life. The evil comes when we begin to build a background or setting for these jewels in the vices and faults of others. When we do this our virtues lose whatever value they otherwise might have and breed discord within ourselves and with those about us. This renders us impotent to help others and dries up the source that feeds our spiritual self.

We abstain from what we consider a bad habit. This abstinence becomes one of our virtues. We ferret out the man who is given to indulgences and proclaim his vices to the high heavens. Do we do this because we want to help this man? No. We want our own virtue to stand out all the more prominently by contrast.

We force ourselves to do a certain thing because doing it would appear to be evidence of an excellent virtue. In order to increase our reward for having sacrificed so much for this virtue, we set out to condemn others who have not adopted it. Thus we acquire the habit of measuring our own worth by comparing ourselves with others.

But we go no further. We seek to help society by selecting an assortment of virtues, and causing those about us to wear them. All of these efforts lead only to bitterness and strife, and end in discouragement and failure.

Harmony with our inner spiritual self leads to the true conception of life. Living in harmony with those about us opens the window through which others may see the light, and eventually the many virtues we sought in vain to establish by force will, because of this light, flourish and make our lives worth living.

The Raw Material of Life

I was fascinated by the operations of a large mill in the mountain country of Idaho. Vast quantities of earth and rock went through the powerful, throbbing machinery. From huge crushers to delicate, sensitive separators went the raw material until, at last, there remained only a few pounds of precious ore.

I marveled that so much raw material produced such little value.

The endless raw material of life is the source from which we glean wisdom.

The miner takes his few pounds of precious ore to the minter who stamps it into coins which people use with little or no thought of the mining process that produced them.

But when a fragment of wisdom is coined from the varied experiences of life and is placed in circulation, what purpose does it serve?

Alas! If wisdom could be separated from the raw material of life and refined into a form that could be used by each succeeding generation with as much profit as came to the person who gleaned it, what a different world this would be!

No. Wisdom is valuable only to the individual who gleans it from the experiences of his own life. Why, then, the almost fanatic zeal with which so many individuals try to force what they believe is wisdom upon others?

This zeal springs from the surge that is inherent in all humans—to shape the thoughts and actions of the masses to the thoughts and actions of the individual. Thus we find the underlying motive that causes many of the present-day crusades even as it caused the crusades of ancient and medieval times.

The instant we learn a lesson from life—a bit of wisdom—we hasten forthwith to impose it upon others, knowing in our heart that when others have lived through certain experiences they will then have learned the same lesson we already have learned, or, in truth, they may live the experience without learning its lesson at all, and thus have lived in vain. We seek to deny others the experiences we have lived and thrust upon them ready-made lessons we ourselves have learned. This entire procedure rests upon a false foundation and visits harm upon those we would help.

The miner who laboriously moves a mountainside through his machinery, works in vain when he fails to glean from the material the wealth that it holds. Such is

worthless, useless motion that saps his strength and gives him nothing in return.

So with living. Through the delicate and sensitive machinery that constitutes our very being there may have passed in full measure the many and varied experiences of life. Yet, it is not the living but what we get out of it, that is important. If yesterday's living has taught us, in a measure, how to live today, then we may face the future without regret, secure in the knowledge that each passing day will find us richer in wisdom and hence possessed of a measure of life's supreme reward.

Our Priceless Possessions

A thought that grew out of a little incident that occurred in the homestead country of western Washington has remained with me through the years and comes to me now as we review the subject of this discourse.

It happened that one of the boys in our class believed the world was flat. The rest of us believed the world was round. There were no libraries in our neighborhood but there was a fairly large one in a nearby town. The argument eventually led us to this library. Being country boys and somewhat timid, we struggled through a great many books before we made known to the librarian the object of our search.

"But," said the boy who believed the world flat, "I don't want any of the books we've seen. They all say the world is round. I want some books that say it is flat so I can prove it to these fellows."

"I am afraid there are no such books in this library," explained the patient librarian.

"Then," said the undaunted defender of a flat world, "we'll have to write to a big library where they do have them."

It didn't occur to this little fellow that possibly his conception of the world's contour was wrong. He proposed to stick to his conviction and diligently search for proof that he was right. He rejected all contrary evidence with the simple but truthful statement that he wasn't looking for anything that might prove he was wrong; he wanted only proof that he was right.

Many of us are like this boy. We have certain very definite notions of what is right and what is wrong; we map out a course we propose to follow with the fixed conviction that it will lead us to the particular goal we have in mind. We then ask our imagination, our inner mind, our will, and every other part of our being to assist us along the course we have chosen to follow. We allow our mind to consider only such information as tends to prove our notions to be right, rejecting all else as not wanted.

We wish certain things to be true; therefore they are true. Under these circumstances we deny ourselves the full value that comes from the proper use of the powers within us.

I once heard a famous man start a speech before an audience of old-time friends in this manner:

"Well, as you all know, I once believed (and he mentioned the beliefs that he once held), but I have lived since then and now I want to confess that I have changed my mind. And today I am certain that I know far less than I thought I knew years ago."

Our most priceless possessions are the fragments of truth we have learned from living. Truth comes before all else. Let us not expect the blessings that come from the use of the ample faculties we all possess until we have freed ourselves of our prejudice, our hatreds, and all manner of hypocrisy that constantly seeks to steal its way into our daily lives.

We know a young lady who has learned three languages and has accumulated an astonishing amount of information from books. She attends most of the worthwhile lectures and seldom misses an opportunity to patronize art exhibits and musical concerts.

Perhaps this girl derives pleasure and satisfaction from these sources. But she seems haunted by a fear that she might miss something; that what she has acquired depends for its value on keeping up to date. She seems distressed when those about her have nothing in common with her, which is most often the case.

But she is also distressed when those about her have more than she of the things she is seeking to acquire. Not that she envies them; but rather that they remind her of the efforts she has not made.

In short, her languages, her books, her art and her music are her masters. She is not master of them.

Hers is an exaggerated case. There is danger that each of us is somewhat like her.

The things in which we find pleasure—our books, our art, our music—all these are necessary elements of life. We cannot grow without them. But we should feed upon them and should not allow them to feed upon us. When we feed upon them we acquire beauty, strength and personality. When they feed upon us we lose all of these.

Sometimes we are willing that they should feed upon us if only they will envelop us completely, for we long for an asylum that will shield us from the hideous discords of commonplace, humdrum living. This is a natural desire but yet an unworthy one that cannot be satisfied. For we cannot escape life except through death.

Let us, then, face life and its many practical everyday problems with the calm assurance that each day we are learning more and more how to live; not how to run away from living. And our diversions—our pleasures, our books, our music, our art—all are elements of the food that sustains us.

In most cases those who seek advice have no clear conception of the true state of affairs whence their troubles arise.

Not long ago I received a letter from one who was struggling with a problem which, he confessed, worried him. He could see no way out. He described in detail, as accurately as he could, just what his difficulties were. But the letter we received from him was not the letter that told of his troubles. Instead, it was a cheerful letter that explained what the first letter was and why he hadn't mailed it.

"When I wrote it all down," he explained, "I realized how unimportant it sounded. It was the first time I ever tried to put in writing the thoughts that were in my mind. And most of them weren't thoughts at all, I guess, because nothing seemed to be real enough to put into words."

The most dangerous part of seeking advice is in relating the details of the problems we have. Just telling them seems to ease our minds and helps us breathe easier, as it were. But we want our story to be convincing, and we allow our imagination to fill in the dramatic details that fact has omitted. In telling our dramatic story often enough we eventually believe it. Continually telling it has the added danger of encouraging us to feel sorry for ourselves and actually to enjoy the pity of others. Instead of trying to eliminate our troubles we spend our time searching for someone to whom we may tell them.

Relief would come by explaining in detail what we intend to do about our problems. Like the man who found that most of his thoughts weren't thoughts at all but dark, sinister fears that whispered to his mind, so at first we would find that the thoughts we have on how to solve our problems aren't thoughts at all, but merely a jumble of fears and hopes that have taken no tangible form.

If one sorely-pressed by trouble would record the fragments of thoughts that dart here and there through his tortured mind for twenty-four hours, he would be amazed at the strange assortment of meaningless words.

Confronted with this tangible evidence that his mind, which alone could help him, had turned traitor and was doing all it could to harass and torture him, he would take stern command of himself and put his mind to work on a sane, practical program of relief. In the absence of anything else, it would be well if he made it repeat, whenever vague fears and doubts seek to enter, a few solid truths. We would suggest these:

No matter what I have done in the past, I have learned from doing it how to live in the future. Therefore, my past will help and not hurt me.

Character is what I am. Reputation is what people think of me. Very well. Let them think anything they may for the present. I am building within me the stuff character is made of and soon character will overcome reputation and people will know me for what I am.

I am constantly striving to live in harmony with my inner self and with those about me. Therefore, I will await the future with the calm assurance that all will be well.

Making a House... a Home

Many people agree with the general theory that the home is the foundation upon which rests the fate of all other social institutions.

Creating and maintaining a real home where children are born and reared is a fine art that should take first place in our daily life. Establishing and maintaining a home is a rare privilege, not a humdrum responsibility that fastens itself like a millstone about our necks and drags us down from the finer things of life.

Home should be the source from which springs all that is worthwhile in life. But, alas, it is the institution that has suffered most from the new and complicated machine age.

Formerly, the home was the end toward which all means were directed. Gradually, we are reversing this and coming to consider the home as merely a means toward many ends that seem to us alluring and worthwhile.

The home is the base of supply that furnishes our inspiration, our hope and our reward. It is our only shelter from the heedless milling multitude that so carelessly tramples us underfoot when we slip and fall. When we undertake an expedition in search of pleasure and reward that leads us further and further from home, we are apt to find ourselves cut off from our base of supply and thus denied the very things for which we have searched.

At Reno, Nevada, the wife of one of America's most successful financiers secured a divorce. Reluctantly she told a story that is becoming all too commonplace. "We have everything in the world," she said, "except a home."

Some wise poet has said: "It takes a deal of living to make a house a home."

Graceful architecture, exquisite furniture and modern comforts form a beautiful setting for a home, but they do not, in themselves, constitute a home.

Harmony of purpose, unselfish devotion to one another, painstaking consideration of each other's worries and cares; these come first. These, in a shack, are to be preferred to discord, selfishness and heartaches in a palace.

I received a long questionnaire from an eastern university asking me, in common no doubt with many others, to express my opinion as to the outstanding American problem.

Without hesitation I gave it as my opinion that the foremost problem in America is "How to make a house a home." Then I hastened to qualify my reply. I did not mean that the average American home is threatened with any-

thing in particular. Neither did I wish to imply that it is any less a home today than it was a few generations back.

What I meant is this: Science and the machine age have wrought miracles in the creation and maintenance of houses, but the art of living has not kept pace. In other words, science and machinery build the house. The art of living alone can convert the house into a home.

Hundreds of thousands of men and millions of dollars constantly are at work seeking to create better and ever better houses. Radios, television, comfortable furniture, heating and cooling systems, and innumerable other devices are continually being improved and brought within the range of the average pocketbook.

But the sole opportunity to create a home belongs exclusively to the people who live in the house.

When there is a short-circuit, we call the electrician who quickly restores the flow of electric current. But when discord and neglect dim the light in mother's eyes, who may restore it?

The carpenter, the plasterer, the paperhanger and others are all at our beck and call to repair or rebuild when the house needs it. But who is there to encourage and comfort father when he finds the going hard and his ability to cope with fast-moving competition weakened?

When we buy a new mechanical device for the house we study the printed instructions carefully. We know that we must follow these instructions or the machine will not work.

There should be a set of general instructions attached to each husband and wife for their individual observance.

Among the instructions given the wife would be:

1. Don't remind your husband, even by subtle suggestion, of the many things others' husbands have provided for their wives that yours has not provided for you. Rather, show a keen and enthusiastic appreciation for the things you have.

2. Don't compare your husband's ability or efforts, to his disadvantage, with those of others. Applaud him for the efforts he makes and he will redouble them. Belittle and scoff at his efforts and he will abandon them.

And these for the husband:

1. Remember you are constantly abroad during the day, mingling with others, gossiping, hearing new ideas. You eliminate the drudgery of your work by having constant contact with others. Thus you grow. Your wife has no such opportunity. Say what you will, washing dishes is washing dishes and housework is housework. If you expect your wife to be your companion she must have an opportunity to grow with you. She, too, needs social contact and diversion. More especially if there are children in the home.

2. When you return home of an evening, don't leave your good humor, your smile and your office manners downtown. Take them home with you.

3. Don't assume the attitude that your wife is eternally indebted to you for board and room. Or that you have discharged your full responsibility toward your home when you have paid the bills.

4. Appreciate the little things your wife does for you. Don't accept them as so much service that is coming to you. At least, be as courteous and kind to your wife as you would be to a stranger.

You Are Master

Today's newspapers contain thousands of news dispatches from all over the world, each intended to add to your store of information. Some will hold your attention for a few hours. Most of them very properly will be discarded as unimportant.

Besides items of news, your newspaper also will present for your amusement and entertainment many special features by highly paid artists and writers. If these features hold your attention for a few moments, they will have fulfilled their purpose.

Yet, if this morning you were to read every page of every newspaper published in the world, you would find nothing more important to you than this:

You are the sole master of your thought processes!

Yesterday's thoughts made you what you are today. Creation is a continuing process. Today's thoughts are creating precisely what you will be tomorrow. Knowing this to be true is one thing. School children for generations have learned penmanship by copying similar truths in their copybooks. Knowing the truth only aggravates the offense against yourself unless you do something about it.

This question frequently is asked: "How may I be sure that I know how to think?" There is no simple, easy answer to this question, but there are certain fundamental truths that may be set forth which, in themselves, will start the process of correct thinking. And thought, once stimulated, develops naturally.

I cannot repeat too often the value of harmony with our inner self and with those about us. Thought is the great harmonizing agency.

James Allen has said, in his immortal essay, "As a Man Thinketh":

> "Mind is the master-power that molds and makes
> And man is mind, and evermore he takes
> The tool of Thought, and, shaping what he will,
> Brings forth a thousand joys, a thousand ills—
> He thinks in secret, and it comes to pass—
> Environment is but his looking-glass."

Much has been written on the subject of thought. Although its great power has won immortal tributes from the wise men of all ages, it presents a fascinating new field for countless students of each succeeding generation.

It is not enough to confine our study to what others have accomplished through thought. We must develop a simple method whereby each of us may profit from the use of the great power within us.

Fortunately, we can start exactly where we are; we do not need to wait until our circumstances have changed.

As you read these words you are conscious of certain mental reservations. You are not quite ready to open your mind completely. Your reasoning faculty insists upon interposing itself between you and your consciousness. For the time being, then, relax completely and let the picture these words are about to present flow freely into your mind.

All nature is in harmony with a fixed law of the universe that does not change. Think of this law as a spirit. Conceive this spirit as you already have visualized wave lengths that enter your radio. This spirit is the only source from which your life may be enriched.

You are a receiving set for this spirit. Believe this, for it is true. Once you marveled that a small instrument called radio could capture the music of a massed orchestra thousands of miles away.

You have within yourself the means of tuning in with the spirit of the universe. Though you are but a grain of sand in the vast realm of the universe, yet the whole universe is within you.

Saying you should learn to develop your power of thought is just another way of saying you should learn how to tune in or harmonize with the spirit of the universe.

Living is merely an endeavor to tune in. Each religion, each creed, each belief points the way. But since no two individuals are alike, it is at once apparent that each individual must tune in for himself. Much despair and discouragement comes from attempting to use the other person's formula. Any or none of them may help you.

Let us carry the illustration further. While each individual receiving set is capable of perfect reception and always has been, yet it also is capable of developing static that will result in utter confusion and lead us to believe there is nothing but confusion and discord available.

The static referred to in this comparison is man-made and unnatural.

Here are some of the things that create static: Hatred and envy; dwelling much upon the faults of others; whining about what others are continually doing to harm you; poisoning the mind and soul by seeking evidence that all about you is wrong and wicked; laying your shortcomings and failures at the doors of others rather than at your own; practicing selfishness by measuring every step and every idea in terms of what it will do for you to the exclusion of all others; taking the punishment of others into your own hands; attributing your temporary success in the world to your own efforts exclusively, thus denying the existence of the only source from which true life satisfaction can come.

So long as we strive to eliminate static we are growing. For each effort at eliminating static puts us that much closer to the point where true harmony begins.

When a man loses his job or fails in business, has his home taken away from him because he cannot pay the rent or the installments on the mortgage, or suffers any one of the many calamities that befall humans, a lot of jumbled, disconnected thinking goes on in his mind.

His friends will talk about his failure. People will point

him out as a man who tried to be somebody and failed.

The nice things he purchased for the home when hope ran high leer at him and say: "You are just like all other failures. You didn't have brains to know your limitations. Now look at the mess you are in. You aren't in our class. We won't be with you long. Better sell us and get through with it."

Thoughts and forebodings torment him. In his mind he builds one case after another in a frantic effort to convince himself that his failure is due to some evil person or some scheme that has been concocted against him. Or perhaps he is the victim of circumstances. Someone was jealous of him, hated him, or envied him. His enemies resorted to tactics that were beneath his own standard of ethics, hence he was utterly defenseless.

Thus does the so-called failure, in "talking things over" with himself destroy the very source of strength that can solve his problems

The one time in every man's life when sound thinking and correct measuring of value is supremely important is when he is experiencing so-called failure. And of all times, this is when his mind is at its worst.

If the failure only realized the truth, he would know that his friends and neighbors aren't thinking about him at all; at least they are not judging him. In the first place, they have serious problems of their own. In the second place, there is a vast difference between idle chatter and serious thought. Idle chatter is a waste of time, and the failure should remember that in the final analysis it harms only the chatterer.

The failure should remember that reputation is only what others think he is—just that and nothing more. Character is what he is. In the long run character overtakes reputation. Therefore, why waste a minute worrying about what people think of him? Rather, he should build character, and some day people will know him for what he is. There always will be reasons for failure. Call the reasons adverse circumstances, envious associates and enemies inspired with hatred and jealousy—or what you will. Any man who proposes to do nothing but feel sorry for himself until the way toward success is cleared of all opposition will lose even the undeveloped ability he now possesses.

The fight back from failure is a grand experience. It is a fight that most any man can win if he wages it intelligently and according to the rules of truth. Many who read this will experience an involuntary feeling of bitterness which finds expression in the reply: "Yes, for the fellow who isn't fighting back, and for the lucky ones who always come out on top. What does the winner really know about the loser?"

We won't quarrel about this. I know, my dear reader, that your problem is different from all others. Just as there are no two individuals alike in all the world, just so no two personal problems are exactly alike. And when I say, "The fight back from failure is a fight most any man can win if he fights intelligently and according to the rules," I do not mean to create in your mind the impression that so-called failure can easily be understood and explained away.

I know that one's health, his environment, his heredity, the peculiar rules and regulations of society under which he lives—all must be taken into consideration in explaining his failure or in accounting for his success.

Society may point to an individual and say: "That person is a complete failure," yet the person to whom society points may be the most contented individual alive. An individual seemingly may occupy the very pinnacles of success, yet, seared deep in his heart, is the feeling that he is in fact an abject failure.

The twinge of conscience, regret, remorse, the feeling of being a failure, or, indeed, the actual realization of apparent failure, are not, after all, evidence of the hopelessness of one's case. Quite to the contrary they constitute genuine, dependable bits of evidence that self-improvement is the way out. And self-improvement is possible for everyone to whom this evidence has been made manifest.

I don't care much for platitudes and slogans. Telling a man who is about to swim that the way to avoid drowning is to stay on top of the water obviously is a waste of words. Telling the failure that the way to improve his condition in life is to improve himself is almost as bad. No man wilfully or deliberately hurts himself. In fact, every man wants to improve himself.

Indeed it is possible that more individuals have been harmed by platitudes than ever have been helped by them.

A man who plunges into the ocean cannot avoid drowning merely by memorizing the words about staying on top of the water. Neither may a failure expect to fight back to success merely by relying upon platitudes and proverbs.

Once I saw a little boy playing with his chemical set. He filled a test tube with some kind of acid. It was clear as crystal, and only upon close examination could I see where the liquid ended and clear air began. Then he added another chemical. At once the liquid became a myriad of crystals, some in the shape of flakes, some that resembled string and others that had the appearance of solid stone. The thought occurred to me that if, by some miracle, the invisible influences that surround each individual could thus be subjected to some chemical treatment and made to stand out in bold relief, what a lesson humanity would learn! There would be one strong cable running back through generations and anchored firmly in the prejudices and physical and mental habits of people long forgotten. If we could see the man straining and pulling against this cable, how different our attitude toward him would be! Too, there would be solid walls all about the individual; walls that he himself never knew existed. We probably would have no names for the walls. But they would be there just the same. Seeing them, very likely we would cease abusing and criticizing the individual for his failure to make more progress.

Then there would be all sorts of threads, strings and ropes running from the individual to other individuals about him. What a shock such a demonstration would be!

Many who little dreamed of the influence they had on others would be surprised to find the ropes attached to themselves! The words and thoughts that suddenly would, in our miracle, be given form, would loom large in the picture. Many would be seen crashing against the man, sorely hurting him. Others would be seen to enter his being and visibly strengthen and help him in his fight.

The failure might set out to readjust society and reconstruct the economic system of the world and live on the hope that he would thus liberate himself and others. He would get nowhere with such a program. Disgusting beyond description is the spectacle of a man spending his

time in an utterly futile effort to reorganize society, while at home his wife and children are forced to live their days in misery and want. There is but one possible way out for the failure. That way is self-improvement.

This conclusion is old and shopworn; it is known by most everyone. Those who know it belong to one of two classes. In the first class are found those who do not care. I will be quite frank and say I am unable to understand the people in this class. In my garden I have observed trees that do not grow and roses that die in the bud. Out of every planting of sweetpeas there are sickly, listless vines that simply do not react to sunshine, cultivation and nourishment.

So, too, with individuals. In every group will be found those who do not desire self-improvement; listless, stupid people in whom the fire of life has never burned.

Then there is the vast throng of men and women in whom the zest for living wells high, even though they find themselves in the mire of failure into which they have been forced through circumstances against which they are struggling. Above everything else these individuals desire to regain solid footing. They crave life satisfaction. It is with these individuals that we are concerned.

The Goal of Truth

We know, of course, the general relation between the food we eat and our physical condition. If we put pain-creating food into our stomach we get very definite and unmistakable returns within a few hours. Even the scoffer and unbeliever admits that poison taken into one's stomach causes distress.

Unfortunately, the effect of poison in the mind is not so generally understood. As a result, we permit poisonous thoughts to enter our minds that affect our mental and spiritual being, exactly as poison food affects our physical system. Suspicion, for instance, may very easily become a poison potent enough to cause failure. A man may have health, personality, ability, imagination and ambition and yet find himself in the mire of failure because he has allowed his mind to become poisoned with suspicions. He sees the executives of the firm with which he is connected in conference. Instantly he suspects they are plotting against him.

He hears a group of fellow employes laughing and the thought overwhelms him that they are laughing at him! He believes the "big fellows" are in league to rob and destroy the "little fellows," or that the "little fellows" are organizing to destroy wealth and property.

He maintains that every man who runs for office has some secret scheme up his sleeve. He regards the street-car conductor as a sly crook, ever on the alert to short-change him. He believes the corner policeman is out to get him. He sees an automobile bearing down upon him. He just knows the driver is deliberately trying to hit him.

At home the suspicious man soon conceives the notion that his wife is unfaithful. When she smiles she is trying to fool him. If she is angry it is because he has been too smart for her and has thwarted her plans.

Finally, the suspicious man loses his position, goes into bankruptcy or otherwise fails. This he regards as final proof that all of his suspicions were well founded. Of course they were not. Suspicion had poisoned his mind and failure was inevitable.

Experts who deal with such matters tell us that at least ten failures out of every hundred are victims of mind-poisoning through over-doses of suspicion, and that every individual whose mind has been poisoned with suspicion eventually becomes a failure.

The cure is slow, but simple and certain. Suspicion cannot live in the clear light of day. It thrives only in the dark secret chambers of the mind. The man who is cursed with an abnormal tendency toward being suspicious is already well on the road toward a cure when he discovers the cause—suspicion—of his troubles.

In the grand experience of fighting back from failure, let us eliminate mind-poisoning caused by suspicion, just as a man afflicted with hay fever would avoid the pollen of goldenrod if he discovered it to be the cause of his distress.

On the bottom of a school report card was this notation —"F—means failure." Just an innocent little word of seven letters, yet it has ruined more lives than probably any other word in the dictionary. Wherever the word is used, it seems to me, there should be a short essay on what it really means. The very utterance, "I am a failure," contradicts itself. For the only man who can qualify as a genuine failure is the man who is unconscious of the fact that he is a failure.

"Failure" is a sort of germ-word that destroys confidence, initiative and self-respect. And this germ-word is carried about and passed on by people who have no idea of the deadly work they are doing. How often a wife thinks she is goading her husband into successful effort by calling him a failure! How often a father chides his son or daughter for failing in work!

The man doesn't live who hasn't failed in many important undertakings. And quite often the man who has accomplished most in the world is the man who has made the greatest number of failures. Failure is not in itself a thing to be proud of, but neither is it a thing to be ashamed of. Learning a lesson from a failure is a noble accomplishment, and upon such accomplishments is so-called success

built. A succession of failures teaches us to think straight, to eliminate preconceived notions and prejudices developed by environment and early training over which we had no control; and above all else, to measure values correctly.

In a sense, life is like a ladder that rests far down in a seemingly bottomless pit, but extends upward farther than any human has ever climbed. Each day of our life is a rung of this ladder, and we build toward the top or the bottom, depending entirely upon which end of the ladder our mind conceives.

In the newspaper press recently there appeared an item concerning a young man who had received notice of dismissal from his university on account of unsatisfactory scholarship. Shocked and bewildered, the boy ended his life with poison.

Undoubtedly parents, teachers and close friends alike were utterly unaware that this unfortunate boy was so tragically sensitive. Yet it does seem that all teachers should have in mind the possibility that each pupil, deep in his heart, is extremely sensitive to criticism, just as he is responsive to praise and encouragement. In this instance the discouraged boy was presented with a brutally blunt printed form that curtly announced his dismissal.

How much better it would have been if someone in authority at the university had called the boy into his office and said:

"My boy, several of the professors who are very much interested in your work tell me they have been unsuccessful in getting their ideas over to you. I'm not at all sur-

prised. You know there are no two of us alike in this world. Each one of us has his own tastes, his own natural tendencies, his individual likes and dislikes. Even brothers aren't alike. The same family may produce a square-jawed man of action who takes to combat like a duck to water; a scientist who cares for nothing but seclusion and study, and a light-hearted poet who craves freedom and the opportunity to interpret love and beauty.

"Standardization is the curse of our age. Your case is just further proof. We all know of famous men who stood out from the crowd. Most of them were failures according to our stupid rules of standardization. But, of course, they weren't. They were just different.

"Unfortunately, our system of education is not flexible enough to be of value to you. You would be foolish to stay here. I want you to read this. It contains the names of men and women who failed in school but who succeeded in life. Among others, you will find some of the most famous names in history. Good-bye and good luck. Just be yourself. Work hard at doing the things you want to do while you are young."

In "The Portrait of a Diplomat" the life interest of Sir Arthur Nicholson is recorded. A few random excerpts illustrate our point. For instance: "Arthur Nicholson was neither imaginative nor intellectual. . . . When he left that school (Rugby) the report . . . ran as follows: 'Your boy has been an absolute failure at Rugby. We can only hope that he will be less of a failure in after life.'"

Later, Nicholson went to Oxford. There, so the report

goes, "They found him indolent, undisciplined and untidy. Nicholson left Oxford without taking his degree. There were debts also . . ."

Again: "He had shirked the navy, failed at Rugby and had not been successful at Brasenose." And yet this man became a world leader; his country honored him. Oxford made him a fellow; and perhaps no man of this century has lived a more interesting and useful life. "What kind of a record am I making with myself?" is a far better question to ponder than "What do other people think of me?"

"What a silly creature," we say of the snake that destroys itself when tormented by an enemy. We think more of the common, skulking rat that backs into a corner and courageously defends itself against overwhelming odds.

Most predatory animals, and practically all birds of prey, are masters of the psychology of fear. The dog weakens his foe with savage barks and growls; the cat with snarls and weird wailings. The hiss of the snake, the scream of the hawk are intended to reduce their prey to helpless, defenseless things. That great hunter, the huge owl of the north, sounds off in the still, quiet air of the forest with such terrifying effect that mice, rabbits and squirrels involuntarily betray their presence to his keen ears.

I feel quite certain that rabbits will never learn to defy the screech of a hawk or the snarl of a bob cat; that mice will never be able to defend themselves against the cruel, piercing whistle of the weasel. But I am utterly at a loss to understand why we exalted human beings, gifted with the ability to think and reason, so often allow ourselves to be destroyed, at least morally and mentally, by noises and circumstances that are creatures of our own making. Bankruptcy, failure, loss of business, loss of position, social obscurity—these are the man-made demons to whom we have given voice. We quail and flutter before their cries like a rabbit before the scream of an eagle. And once in the clutches of any one of them we give up our self-confidence, our courage, our sense of humor, and most everything else save bare physical existence.

Snap out of it! In this mad whirl of life no man is broken until he betrays himself and does things which he himself knows, at the time he does them, to be downright crooked and wrong. And even then there is hope for the man who knows he has done wrong and sets out to go straight. There is genuine complete success in honest failure; there is nothing but complete failure in dishonest success.

From reading the many pamphlets, books and letters that inevitably come to an editor's desk, I am impressed with the astounding amount of thought that is devoted to ideas and plans for removing the hurdles from the path of life. Of course there are hurdles in the way. The sex problem, the food problem, the problem of rearing and caring for our young, the struggle against the elements, the struggle of man against man—all these are hurdles that stand across the roadways of life.

Why allow this fact to discourage us? The very purpose of life is to pass through the experience of conquering hurdles. When we understand this truth and develop our thinking in harmony with it, we will acquire courage and stamina sufficient to carry us to the end of the journey.

Unfortunately, however, many individuals deny this truth and develop the conviction that the greatest possible service to humanity consists in removing the hurdles themselves, in condemning a scheme of life that employs barriers and obstacles, and in exhorting mankind to organize an improved plan wherein the great god Ease will reign supreme.

So far such efforts have failed. For every hurdle that has been removed, countless new ones have sprung up. Are we, then, condemned to a continuous life of trouble, strife and disappointment? If we are to accept the truth as we have experienced it, and as it has been handed down to us through the ages, we must admit that these will always be on one side of the ledger in every life record; but on the other side will be genuine satisfying rewards that life has to offer.

All this may seem well and good to the individual who has been able to surmount the obstacles before him, but what of the countless thousands who have tried and failed? Who knows? Without hurdles, life would hold no interest; it would be devoid of every quality that makes for satisfaction; it would offer no incentive for progress and would be much like our present conception of death.

The lot of the so-called failure is far from hopeless. Each life is a part of eternity and represents a continuation of a journey. No worthy effort is in vain, and all failure is but a step nearer the goal of Truth.